54 Questions for the Man Who Sold a Shotgun to My Father

Joe Carrick-Varty

Out-Spoken Press
London

Published by Out-Spoken Press,
Unit 39, Containerville
1 Emma Street
London, E2 9FP

The rights of Joe Carrick-Varty to be identified as the author of this
work have been asserted by them in accordance with section 77 of the
Copyright, Designs and Patents Act 1988.

A CIP record for this title is available from the British Library.

First edition published 2020
ISBN: 9781838021139

Typeset in: Adobe Caslon

Out-Spoken Press is supported using public funding by the National
Lottery through Arts Council England.

Supported using public funding by
**ARTS COUNCIL
ENGLAND**

Acknowledgments

Thanks are due to the editors of the publications where some of these poems, or versions of them, first appeared: *The Interpreter's House*, *Magma*, *Manchester Review*, *New Statesman*, *PN Review*, *Poetry Ireland Review*, and *Poetry Review*. Special thanks to Anthony Anaxagorou, Rowland Bagnall, Patricia Ferguson, Ella Frears, Elizabeth Garrett, Wayne Holloway-Smith, Gboyega Odubanjo, Anne Varty and Mariah Whelan.

Contents

And God said 1

Sambas for Christmas 2

Dear Postie 3

When he waits at the bar my father's brain is
miles above his pint 4

Withdrawal 6

THE CHILDREN 7

More Sky 10

The Father Heavens 11

           Father Cosmology

           Fathers of Previous World Cycles

           Great Peacock Wisdom King

           Life Father

All my fathers are hunting dodos in the park 15

54 Questions for the Man Who Sold a Shotgun
to My Father 16

Lamech 18

There's a Person Reflected on the TV Calling
Their Dad 19

here are the woods here are birds
here is sunlight here is leaf and branch
here are paw prints here is lichen
here is rain and air and sunlight
here are berries and blood here is leaf
here is gurgle of stream and skull
of moose here are paw prints
here is foxglove here are birds
here is fur on branch here is rain
here is sunlight here are paw prints
here is air here is moose half-eaten
here is pine here is elm no birds
for hours no birds here is pool
look my father how he floats
listen how his bear drinks

And God said

Every time a horse lies down in a sunlit field
an island goes up off the coast of Alaska or Peru
or in the middle of a lake south of Stockholm.
Every time a whale is born albino
a man doesn't die of liver failure and every time
it rains at sea a child speaks first words.
Every time you watch the football
in your alcoholic father's flat
on his little settee that unfolds into a bed
in case you ever wanted to stay
a forest disappears and a doorbell rings.
Every time the ref blows the whistle
and your father boils the kettle and somewhere
islands are going up and oil rigs just watching.

Sambas for Christmas

In a corner of some far-flung town
on some moon of some planet
at the edge of some pocketed galaxy
the soles of my father's new trainers
are landing on tarmac, squeaking
as they take off again, box-fresh
at the end of his faded black jeans.
They will squeak for a week or so
and then he will die on his back
in his sleep like Jimi Hendrix
after a night at a pub that's not quite my local
whistling as he stumbles home
running his fingers through a rosemary bush
awash in the chippy's neon blue.
Believe, for a minute, that I am not a son
who buys trainers for his father
but a molecule of gas inside a star
whose light still touches a city
that's not quite Oxford where a father
who's not quite mine tries on pairs
of Adidas, Nike, struggling with the laces,
the incomprehensible bow.

Dear Postie

If no answer please leave parcel behind rhododendron—
if storm hits and rhododendron blows away
please leave parcel inside wheelie bin with brick on top—
if crying baby can be heard on approach
tap three times on bottom-left panel of shed window—
DO NOT ring doorbell—if rainbow windmill
spins slower than usual open phone and call alcoholic father—
if rainbow windmill stops spinning at any moment
come back in month with picture of alcoholic father
eating fish and chips in park—if phone rings out
wait for nesting swallows to return from Africa
then call again—DO NOT mention alcoholic father
to friends colleagues woman you love—DO NOT
kiss woman you love—DO NOT eat sleep
shit watch TV until alcoholic father is spotted
leaving Tesco with Guinness and Hula Hoops—
DO NOT I repeat DO NOT drive to 24-hour Shell garage
spend following afternoon outside alcoholic father's flat
old ladies watching—bay windows blue with Countdown.

When he waits at the bar my father's brain is miles above his pint

like the swimming pool
I watch six cranes
lower onto the roof
of a skyscraper as
my father gets drunk
with a man called Gary
the kind of drunk
you can peer into
their earrings glinting
their hearts a pair of
tiny red whales
I watch the builders fit
three whole floors
with windows
one guy comes out
carrying a fox
dangles it Michael Jackson-
style over the lip
of a balcony my father
cannot remember
the name of the film
the score of the game
sometimes I drink
and lie and tell strangers
in pub gardens
that my father

is being built that
he's coming back
from the ground
that I'll pull a fox
out of his body one day
carry it in my arms
blinking and pissing
to a sunlit table
just like this one

Withdrawal

Unpack tins of soup—open windows—
scrape grease from the hob—
sync your breathing with his—walk
with purpose between the bathroom
and the light-filled kitchen—
find a moth and let it live—postcards
in a drawer—pictures of a holiday—on the carpet
build a house out of tins—a family—
trees dotted around a pond—
a swallow's nest like the backdoor of a star—
a note on the table you'll soon cycle away from
your fingers like prunes and smelling of bleach.

THE CHILDREN

on the muted screen a ball lands
one side of a line
and this means that a person has won
the camera jiggles
zooms out refocuses on a crowd
who are cheering
which means that a person has won
yes clapping
back smacking drink dropping
all signifiers
that yep a ball has landed
one side of a line
one side not one side but ONE
SIDE of course right
because a person has won
a ball has landed
people are happy and although this is not
a metaphor for grief
I cannot deny that a ball not a ball but
THE BALL
has landed is landing will land
until it stops being
THE BALL and starts being a ball
at the edge of
a roofless room lots of people are
jumping around in-
side of lots of sound lots of screens

lots of open sky and
did I mention my dad has taken a
shotgun to a field
and I haven't realised because I am
watching tennis
which means my dad has decided
is deciding
will decide to become not a dad
but THE DAD
is asking a man for a shotgun is
saying can I buy
yes bring me this much and it's a
man from the pub
someone I'll walk past for years
which means I am
existing in relation to this moment
my sister is
eating a choc ice romping around
the garden holding
a toad in relation to this pocket of
time my mum
zipping up our puffer jackets pulling
down our hats
while my dad walks through rain
to an ATM
leaves a room with a shotgun in a
duffle bag
this moment almost encased in
glass
this skyscraper I am not really watching

tennis inside of
not on my lunch break not
twenty six
but nine years old being pulled out of
maths
my sister four whole years
barely taller
than a table and we are not children
anymore
but THE CHILDREN THOSE CHILDREN
THAT CHILD

More Sky

Have you ever had that thing when a building
gets demolished, a building you walk past every day,
a big but inconspicuous building,
a building you've never properly looked at,
couldn't draw from memory, guess
its number of windows, the impression of a building,
the colour of sandstone in your periphery
as you hurry into afternoons, interviews,
christenings and all of a sudden it's gone,
there's just sky where that building used to be
and you're a mess with your child's bike helmet?

The Father Heavens

After Buddhism *at the British Library, 25 October 2019 – 29 February 2020*

Father Cosmology

This cosmological map depicts the heavenly
realm called 82a Wytham Street with palaces, gardens
and marketplaces for the 33 fathers who reside there.
In the middle is the settee of the father
Daniel who is lord of this heaven. See
the hot rock hole, the ancient shape of a backside.
Take a seat. Oh, you've done that before. This is one
of six heavens or celestial realms.

Fathers of Previous World Cycles

In the Theravāda tradition, four fathers are believed
to have attained Nirvana. The history of these fathers
is given in a text which is traditionally read
to sons in the bath. Kukusandha father
(top) is the first father, Koṇāgamana is the second
father, Kassapa is the third father and the
historical father Daniel born as Our Prince Danny
is the fourth and final father of this era. Every
father has always achieved enlightenment
in the shadow of a certain tree.

Great Peacock Wisdom King

This manual contains paintings of altars for
sons who will one day become fathers
and may end up alone in a flat or may not.
One father can be seen riding a peacock, a bird that
keeps a territory free from snakes. Can you spot
the note left three years ago saying *I've hoovered?*
Yes, a faint smell of skin and Hula Hoops. On the right
a father appears in a stylised wheel. Between
the spokes are the names for certain kinds of shadow.

Life Father

Fatherhood is described as a series of manifestations
that are impermanent. It is thought that there
is no ultimate reality in things—every father
is subject to change and to some extent
dependent (dep / en / dent) on perception.
Sonhood does not encourage
belief in a creator deity or
supreme being. However, where
have you walked to this Sunday morning?
Get up from this settee. Close that empty fridge.
See the years of letters at the door?
Gather them up.

All my fathers are hunting dodos in the park

and I'm watching through an attic's round window
as one of my fathers, dressed in balaclava
and green camo, commando-crawls
across the tennis court while another

crouches behind a wheelie bin, whispers
to himself, cheek paint smudged,
a grenade clutched to his breast.
Gun fire across the boating pond.

Bullets rip the water. One of my fathers
has broken his leg, snaps a branch
for a splint. Another has climbed a tree.
An explosion and a wheelie bin goes flying.

I ask myself if hunt is even the right verb.
I have never seen a real dodo
and neither have any of my fathers.
No, my fathers are killing my fathers in the park

and I'm watching through an attic's round window.

54 Questions for the Man Who Sold a Shotgun to My Father

Is tea an exact science / Are willow trees categorically sad / Can a house have a face / Are astronauts real / How many bad things have been witnessed by just deer / Is hiking peaceful / Are skyscrapers pretty / Was there an imposter at the wake / What does flamingo taste like / Are bees kind / Is the BBC right / Do lemmings understand / Are children who lose a parent to suicide more likely to die the same way / How many kettles are whistling right now / How many tractors will break down today / What did the first nectarine smell of / Where are all the dead ducks / Do whales dream / How many Boeing 737s have successfully landed since 2002 / How old is the oldest tree in Alaska / Which shade of orange was your son's bedroom this morning / How many rivers are there between my body and yours / Is stilton your favourite cheese / Have you ever been to Budapest / Do you have an opinion on Coldplay / Do you remember your ninth birthday / Do you fly well / Do you burp more often than you think you should / Are you hairy / How many mugs have you dropped / Have you ever stroked an elephant / At what age did you stop believing in Santa / How many weddings have you attended / Do you enjoy French films / Have you ever been operated on / Is your garden south-west facing / Do you own a pair of secateurs / Would you call yourself a family man / Were you ever any good at tennis / Is your penis longer than mine / Does it rain in your weather / Is there a bus / Are you waiting by the frozen fruit in Aldi / Wearing a beanie /

Listening to Eminem / Did he tell you what he wanted it for / Did you ask / Did he smile / Did you touch / Talk much / Had he shaved / If you could use a number to describe his laugh would you use 1000 or 3 / Did you put the money towards a loft extension / Is that a lasagne in your oven?

Lamech

I ask my father to die under my breath
in the back of a cab on a Saturday afternoon
traffic at a standstill both ways, the pair of us
heading for a cinema like normal people.
I ask the driver to take us back. Back to the pub?
I shake my head, begin to name things
tree car cloud streetlamp, pull my father down
onto my lap, stroke his bald head
look I say a park children are playing
listen I say it has started to rain.

There's a Person Reflected on the TV Calling their Dad

The seagulls are circling, calling their dads,
the rain is calling its dad and so is the sun
and what's left of the lawn, a skyscraper
is kneeling and calling its dad, a bus, a train,
a city is calling its dad, the mouth
of an underground station opening, Halloween
has called, Christmas will call soon enough
and that new year climbing over the back wall
through the screen door is, of course,
calling its dad. I stand in a room and call my dad,
tell his answer machine not to worry anymore,
that they have found his body.

Other titles by Out-Spoken Press

Lasagne • WAYNE HOLLOWAY-SMITH

Mutton Rolls • ARJI MANUELPILLAI

Contains Mild Peril • FRAN LOCK

Epiphaneia • RICHARD GEORGES

Stage Invasion: Poetry & the Spoken Word Renaissance
PETE BEARDER

Nascent • VOL 1: A BAME ANTHOLOGY

Ways of Coping • OLLIE O'NEILL

The Neighbourhood • HANNAH LOWE

The Games • HARRY JOSEPHINE GILES

Songs My Enemy Taught Me • JOELLE TAYLOR

To Sweeten Bitter • RAYMOND ANTROBUS

Dogtooth • FRAN LOCK

How You Might Know Me • Sabrina Mahfouz

Heterogeneous, New & Selected Poems
ANTHONY ANAXAGOROU

Titanic • BRIDGET MINAMORE

Email: press@outspokenldn.com